D1799639

Telephone Collection call Scripts & How to respond to Excuses

A Guide for Bill Collectors
Part of the Collecting Money Series

By Michelle Dunn

www.MichelleDunn.com
www.Credit-and-Collections.com

Table of Contents

What is the FDCPA

Resources

Introduction

I wrote this book because making collection calls seems to be the scariest part of being a bill collector. As someone who has made thousands upon thousands of debt collection calls as a credit manager and first party collector and as an agency owner and third party collector, I wanted to share what I know about making these calls so that you can improve on your calls. To take the fear out of it, just remember that making a collection call is like making a customer service call. You are calling about a problem with the account and you just want to resolve it.

You will learn what common excuses people give and what you can say to them in order to keep the call moving in the right direction and not going off track. You will learn how to notice a red flag with an account that you are calling and be able to avoid disaster by taking specific steps based on your knowledge of what is happening with that particular account.

This book will help anyone who owns a business and needs to call customers that are past due. It will help accounts receivable clerks who make calls to delinquent accounts; it will help credit managers who make collection calls or "your account is on credit hold" calls. This book will also help collectors who work for a third party collection agency. This book is meant to be a guide for bill collectors.

I have shared with you actual and specific steps I have taken in my years of doing collection work that have worked well for me. I have found that when making collection calls and dealing with excuses, you must be firm, tread lightly, have compassion and treat the account carefully. Treat the account (not the customer) like a child who needs your guidance and help to get this paid. This has worked very well for me and I have successfully collected more money than other collectors based on following these steps.

Part 1 Collection Calls

If you are reading this book chances are you call people for money, or you will have to soon and you are trying to figure out how to do it.   In my years of working in this industry, the biggest question I still see from businesses, new collectors and managers, is how to make the collection call easier, less scary, shorter and more effective. I have a couple of networking groups on LinkedIn, The Guide to Getting Paid and Starting a Collection Agency and have some good discussions going on with the members about ways to make the collection call easier, more effective, less scary and all the things everyone is afraid of.   Check them out once in a while for new information that can help you with your calls.

The best way to become better at making collection calls and dealing with objections is to just keep making the calls. As I did this day in and day out I became better at it, just because of the experience. When you call people all day every day or for long periods of time, you start to see patterns, you will be able to identify red flags and know to take action on those flags in order to get paid. You become familiar with common excuses and can easily respond to them with solutions to help get your bill paid. In my experience, it was the experience of actually making calls, getting through tough calls successfully and being able to move on to the next call by keeping it business and not taking anything personally.

Listening to other bill collectors make collection calls is also very helpful. I found this helped me learn different things I could say, or solutions I could offer, or just gave me a different perspective. When I trained the collectors for my agency, before they could ever make calls, I had them listen to me make calls. This way they know what they can and cannot say, they can ask questions when you hang up, and it is a learning experience for them.

Reading about making collection calls also helped me, there are a few books out there that talk vaguely about it but they are helpful. Also, try to find some customer service scripts, those can also be helpful. As a business making your own collection calls, your credit department is a part of customer service, so you are making a customer service call about getting paid. You can use customer service phone scripts to help you make your debt collection calls.

Before you make Collection Calls

Part of the fear people have about making collection calls, is that they see an account is past due, they get annoyed and pick up the phone filled with that emotion and dial the customer. That is the wrong way to make a collection call, and you will most certainly fail. You may get paid, but could lose a customer or not even get paid and lose a customer. Never make a collection call when you are emotional about the account or debt.

Before you make a call, look up the customer's order history and payment history, check their terms and their credit application, when was the last time you checked their credit? Could their credit limit be too high or too low? Is this the first time they are past due or is this a pattern? When was the last order placed? When was the last time they paid you and how much did they pay? Know the history of the account before you pick up the phone.

Know who you are going to ask for when the phone is answered, you want to talk to the person who signs the checks or pays the bills. This might be the person who signed the credit application, or someone else. Get that person's name if you don't have a specific name when you call, if they have an extension or another number, get that information and make a note on the account.

As you sit at your desk ready to make your first collection call, your computer screen has the customer's account up on it, you have your aging report or copies of the PO's or invoices in front of you, you know the number you are going to dial and who to ask for. You also know the last time this customer placed an order, and the last time you received a check from them. You feel confident and ready. You have all the information you need and a couple of solutions in mind if the customers gives you any objections to paying. Slowly, you reach out and you pick up the phone….

Your Pre-call plan

…you dial and someone answers the phone. You immediately identify the customer to make sure you have the correct person on the phone. You identify yourself by stating your first and last name and the name of your company. Then you tell them why you are calling and ask for payment in full, you stop and you listen. Do not break the uncomfortable silence you may be experiencing right now. Just wait.

Once the customer answers you that is the time when you move on to the next part of the call which I will cover later. First we want to focus on the details of this pre-call plan. The pre-planning of the collection call begins when you review a customer's account and history. You need to start thinking about payment plans that you are authorized to offer this customer, and get authorization before you make the call. You also need to have a solution or two in mind if this customer can't pay off the debt in 2-3 payments. You want to have a couple of things in mind so that when you are on the call you and your customer will have a couple of different options.

An example of a pre-call plan for a first party collector could be:

Hello, may I speak to Anna Smith? This is Michelle Dunn from ABC Company. (Anna gets on the phone) Hi Anna, this is Michelle Dunn from ABC Company calling about your balance due of $150.00 on invoice # 123. I am calling to find out if this invoice has been processed and the check mailed? STOP and wait and listen.

Some things Anna might say and how you can respond:

Excuse #1

Anna: We didn't receive invoice #123…..

You: We sent a copy in the box with your order; did you receive your order?

OR

You: No problem, I am faxing invoice #123 over right now, can you run over to your fax machine and get it while I hold on?

OR

You: No problem, I am just leaving for lunch and will come by and drop it off, can you have a check ready and waiting for me to pick up?

OR

I am just sending it to you attached to an email right now, can you check your email?

Excuse #2

Anna: The price on invoice #123 doesn't match our PO so I can't process this for payment.

You: I have a copy of your PO#432 here and you listed an incorrect price of $1.00 each when the correct price is $1.25 each. How can we correct your PO?

OR

You: Did you receive the order? (Anna says yes) Great, can you process the invoice for the amount you are not disputing in the meantime? I will fax over a copy of our pricing agreement and the invoice. (Many times companies have special pricing that they agree to and have signed contracts to support this.)

Excuse #3

Anna: The check is on Frank's desk to be signed, he just hasn't signed it yet and he is out today.

You: Can I have Frank's direct number so I can leave him a voice mail? Get the number and call Frank and leave a message. Then pull out your credit application or contract and see who signed that, then give that person a call. Create some urgency about the payment so that it gets priority.

AND/OR

You: contact the salesman who made the sale and get that person involved in helping you to get paid.

Excuse #4

Anna: I do have the invoice but we are in a cash crunch and I don't know when it will be paid.

You: Anna, I am sorry to hear that, but I have to report to my boss or supervisor this afternoon and let them know your intentions in regards to this past due invoice, so let's come to an agreement on payment for this balance so that I can let them know your intentions at our meeting. Otherwise, your account will escalate out of my hands and my boss will be giving your boss a call about it.

OR

You: Can you send a partial payment towards this invoice today so I can let my supervisor know you have made a payment towards this balance? Ask for 80% of the balance and work your way down from there. Confirm the payment agreement, and send a confirmation letter.

An example of a pre-call plan for a third party collector:

Anna: I can't believe a collection agency is calling me, I never received that invoice!

You: I am faxing or emailing a copy to you now as we speak, I'll hold on while you get that.

Anna: There was a dispute with that invoice, which is why it was never paid.

You: What was the dispute, why didn't you ever tell the creditor? Why haven't you paid the un-disputed amount? Can I take your payment of the undisputed amount over the phone now?

Anna: They billed us for the incorrect price, and never submitted a corrected invoice, so it has not been paid.

You: I am faxing/emailing over a copy of the PO with the price and a proof of delivery, I'll hold on while you get that.

Anna: We would need a credit for $50 in order to process this invoice, with this wrong pricing on it.

You: I will get back in touch with (Creditor), in the meantime can you send me a check (or pay over the phone) the undisputed balance for products you have received? This would be the balance less the $50 disputed item. Once you get a payment over the phone or a promise, confirm the payment plan, and that you will go back to the creditor about the disputed $50 and give them a call back. If they are sending a check, get a check number and confirm the dollar amount.
You: Immediately hang up and call the original creditor about the dispute. Find out the problem and call the customer back. Don't wait, you want to clear this up today and get it off the books.

OR

Anna: We did not receive that, I know you have a proof of delivery, but we didn't get it.

You: Since we show you did receive it and Frank Smith signed for this on 4/1/2013, we do need to get paid for this bill. Do you have a Frank Smith that works there?

Anna: We refuse to pay that.

You: I will let the Creditor know, in the meantime, be advised that this may be reported to your credit report, or the client/boss may decide to take legal action. I will give them a call and then call you back to let you know what action we will be taking.

You: Call the client; see what they want to do. If you are going to report the debt to the credit bureau, call the customer back and let them know. Many times this will prompt them to pay it. I always sent a confirmation letter that day letting them know that if the balance is not paid by the next Friday, (be very specific, put Friday, and the date) that the debt will be reported to the credit bureau. Then make sure to report it if they do not pay. You can use my letter specifically worded for this instance and for the confirmation letter in my book "The First book of Collection Agency letters and forms" available on Amazon as a paperback or kindle book.

The pre-planning of your call is when you review the customer's account and history as well as their payment history. You will think about re-payment plans you can offer this customer or solutions to any excuse or objections so that when you are on the call you have a couple of different options. Before you dial you will make sure you know who the right person is to talk to and ask for that specific person. This could be the person who signed the credit application or contract or the person who placed the order or the owner of the company. Enlist the sales person who made the sale as a last resort.

Opening Remarks

Once you have a plan in place you want to work on your opening remarks, this will become a habit to you, normally you end up saying the same thing for each call. Your opening remarks are designed to let the customer know right away, who you are, who you are calling for (if you are a third party collector), what company you are calling from, and what you are calling about. When someone answers the phone, that is your window of opportunity to get all of this information to them.

Your opening remarks could be:

Is this Robert Smith? (Yes)

Hi, this is Michelle Dunn from ABC Company or ABC Collection Agency calling for North Shore Vet Hospital (if you are a third party collector).

I am calling about your balance of $1500.00 on invoices 1, 2 and 3 which is past due. I am calling to take your payment over the phone now for this bill, would you like to pay with Visa or MasterCard? STOP. Wait and listen.

Depending on the response, you will have to overcome any objections or excuses they give you. Once you have done that, you will need to set a payment date and get an agreement from the customer as to how much that payment will be, when it will be mailed and what will happen if you don't receive it by the date promised.

Once you have a payment agreement, which is the body of your call, you will move into the closing of your call. But first you want to reiterate to the customer the payment agreement in great detail and then send them a confirmation letter the same day. An example:

You: Robert, let me make sure I have this right, you will send me $100 tomorrow, check #43 and then a check every Friday for $100.00 until September when the balance should be paid in full if you don't miss any payments and make all of these payments on time? Is that correct?

Customer: Yes.

You: Great, this will not be reported to the credit bureau or forwarded to legal as long as we receive your payments. If you miss a payment and do not call me, your account will be out of my hands and forwarded to legal or my boss. Hang up. Send the confirmation letter. Make a note in your computer to call this customer on Thursday before each payment is due to ask for the check number and to verify the check will be sent the next day, Friday. You will probably only have to do this babysitting for a couple of payments. In my experience, people get very tired of you calling to verify the payment is going to be sent, and will start sending it on time or even early just to avoid your call.

The Meat of the Call

As you make collection calls and customers give you excuses or reasons why they cannot pay, you will learn to recognize those excuses as signs. When someone is giving you excuses or objecting in any way, that is the time you need to do something. If you don't know how to respond to a specific excuse or objection, check your company credit policy and talk to your manager. Remember when you are calling customers like this you want to re-evaluate their credit worthiness and their credit limits. Another thing you can do is visit the customer if they are close to you. If you can't realistically visit the customer, call them and talk with them as if you were there in person. This extra attention will go a long way and help limit your risk. The important thing here is that you have to do something and not wait.

Specific actions you can take right now are, re-evaluate their credit, when was the last time you checked their credit? Things may have changed financially for this company and lowering their credit limit could end up helping them stay current and helping you limit that risk. Another thing you could do, if you are aware of your credit policy steps, is when someone is 60 days past due and not giving a payment promise, maybe your policy is that the next step would be to put them on credit hold. So be prepared when you call to let them know if they cannot give you a payment over the phone or promise to mail a payment today their account will be put on credit hold. Once you hang up send the customer a confirmation letter.

The meat of your call is where you will have to determine your approach based on the customers response, or if this is the first call or maybe the 9th call. You will have to listen and respond to any excuses or objections why they cannot pay anything, you will have to work with them to come up with a payment amount and date and get the customer to agree to that arrangement.

If you are doing business to business collections ask for accounts payable or the book keeper. Identify yourself by giving your first and last name, your company name or the company you are calling for or representing. State why you are calling and ask them if they have processed your invoice #123 for payment. Listen to any objections or excuses and then answer those excuses. Once you have answered the objection, to stay on track say something such as, "Russ, I have to report back to my supervisor today on your balance, please let's agree on something I can tell him/her regarding your account. Can you send a partial payment of $(give specific amount based on the balance) today?" Depending on what this customer owes you, start asking for payment in full and then go down to 80% of the total bill and go down from there. Confirm the payment agreement details on the phone hang up and send a confirmation letter.

Closing the Call

Always end your call by going over what you agreed to during the call. You want to repeat everything to the customer to make sure you both agree. For example,

You: That sounds good. You will mail a check for $100 tomorrow, June 5th after work and then $100 every Friday thereafter until your balance due of $400.00 is paid.

Once you say this and hang up the phone, you want to send a letter confirming this agreement. Be very specific, and list out each Friday and the date that each payment will be made. You can find letters like this on the CD in the *Ultimate Credit and Collections Handbook*, or in my books of letters and forms. If possible include a postage paid payment envelope or a payment envelope without postage. You could also include a link on the letter that they can visit to pay online.

It is also a very good idea to tell the customer when you are on the phone what will happen if they do not make the payment as agreed and then include that in your confirmation letter. This would be whatever the next step is in your credit policy process, maybe the account is to the point that if you don't have the payment by a specific date the account will be taken to legal, or reported to the credit bureau, or merchandise repossessed.

Following Up

You started following up when you sent out your confirmation letter to the customer to confirm your agreement and get the first payment. The next thing you want to do is make a note to call that customer on Thursday since they are supposed to mail this payment on a Friday. You always want to call the day before they are to make a payment, especially with the first payment of any payment plan. When you call on Thursday you want to say something similar to:

You: This is Michelle calling from ASP Company about the check for $100 you are going to send me tomorrow. I just wanted to call to confirm that you will be mailing that out to me tomorrow.

You can then repeat your mailing address and/or ask if they received your confirmation letter with the postage paid payment envelope, if enough time has passed since you mailed it.

An example:

If you call a customer on a Tuesday and they tell you they will mail you a check on Friday when they get paid; hang up the phone and send the confirmation letter.

Call them on Thursday to verify the check will be mailed tomorrow.

Call them on Friday to verify the check was actually mailed.

Call them on Tuesday when you don't have the payment.

If you receive the payment as agreed, you want to send the customer a "thank you for your payment" letter. This letter just thanks them for the $100 payment towards their balance due of $5000 and outlines the schedule for the remaining payments, as well as giving them their new balance due. You can also include another postage paid envelope for that next payment.

I know this seems like babysitting, but I have had great luck collecting this way. In my experience, I have found that when you "train" an account this way, it really cuts down on the babysitting you have to do later. It sets a precedence so what seems like a lot of work in the beginning really does pay off later and you don't have to keep it up forever.

Common Excuses

There are so many excuses and objections that customers will say to you as you make collection calls. If you can be prepared for any excuse you will be much more effective. You need to have a response ready for any excuse so that you can reach your goal of getting paid from this customer. Many of the excuses on this list are actual excuses I have been told over the years making collection calls, others have been told to me by others who work in the field. I started out with some business to business excuses and then consumer debt excuses.

Business to Business excuses:

We didn't budget your bill for this year
The invoice has to be approved by another department
We are waiting for our customers to pay us so we can pay you
We did not order this
We did not receive the order
The check is on (somebody's) desk waiting to be signed, and they are on vacation
The book keeper is sick or on vacation
The computer is down
Your invoice is not on my list
I don't have your invoice
Accounts Payable only takes calls on Tuesdays between 1 and 3
The check is ready to mail it just hasn't been signed yet
I fired my contractor so I don't have a building to work out of
I brought you a check and your office staff wouldn't take it because something didn't match
Our company checks were stolen during a robbery so I am waiting for new checks from the bank
I am operating at a loss
My biggest customer just filed bankruptcy
We just changed banks and don't have checks yet

We are too busy to pay our bills right now
We are growing faster than we planned and don't have enough capital
We are having cash flow problems right now

Consumer debt excuses:

The check is in the mail
I already paid that or I thought I already paid that
I don't have any money
I'm divorced and my ex-husband/wife is supposed to pay that bill
I didn't receive all the items I ordered
There was a problem with the order
I suddenly got sick and have medical bills to pay so I can't pay you
I lost my job
My wife/husband handles the bills
I'll try
You are harassing me
I'll pay in full when I get my Christmas club money, tax return, win the lottery
Hold on a minute – then they hang up
I can't get a loan or borrow the money to pay you
My insurance company should have paid that
When I have some extra money, I'll pay you
I have more important bills to pay
I'm filing for bankruptcy
I lost my glasses and can't read my bills or the letters you sent me
My car is broken down and the nearest mailbox is 10 miles away
That person is deceased, and when you call back a week later that person is not home right now
I didn't know I had to pay that
I was robbed of my mail at the post office while trying to mail your check
I can't find my check book but when I do, I will send you a check
I am waiting for it to stop raining
I'm sick, I can't pay anything

I was in a bad car accident and lost my memory
Our dog chewed up all our checks
I hurt my leg playing ball and can't get to the phone, post office, bank
I don't pick up the call when I hear your voice on my machine
I didn't receive the order (even though POD's prove it was delivered)
I didn't receive the invoice (even though it has been sent multiple times)

In my groups on LinkedIn, The Guide to Getting Paid and Starting a Collection Agency, there are many discussions going on that relate to the above excuses. Check out my groups to see how other collectors are responding to these excuses, for more ideas on what you can do and say.

Collection Call Scripts & How to Respond to Excuses

I had to put these two things together because you respond to the excuses when you are on the collection call. Your collection call script and how to respond to any excuses go hand in hand.

Here are some responses to some of the most common excuses that we have been talking about. They may not work in every situation but can work in many and will give you a feel of how to respond in a positive and constructive way that helps you to get paid.

If a customer tells you that they don't have any money or any money coming in to pay you, some things you might respond with could be:

Consumer debt:

Do you really mean that you have no money at all? If this is a consumer debt, talk to them about community help programs they may be eligible for.

Have you applied for unemployment benefits? When will you get your first check?

I'm sorry to hear that. How are you paying your bills? Note that some people will then say that their significant other is paying everything since they don't have any money coming in. You could respond to that by asking if they could start a small payment plan or asking about any job interviews and then calling after the interviews and following up that way.

What are you going to do? What is the plan? Will you apply for unemployment, sell everything and move in with parents, get a new job?

Are you looking for a job? Have you applied anywhere? When will you hear back from them? Have you gone on any interviews?

Business debt:

Is it more of a case of cash flow problems? Let them know about training, books or ways they can collect from their past due accounts, or give them a referral to use your collection agency.

How much are you short? Once they give you a figure you can work on offering a payment plan and get a payment for the amount they do have on hand.

Have you asked the bank for a loan?

What steps are you considering to resolve this situation?

What is the status of your business right now?

The next objection is when a customer tells you not to worry you will be paid or asks you why you are calling them, saying you don't trust them. Many times they become defensive right away and it is harder to deal with them. Some responses you could try:

Responses for consumer debt:

It's not a question of trust; we just need to be paid for the product you are already using.

We are not worried about being paid eventually; we are worried about being paid on time. (Or now)

You trusted us to ship you the product on time at the right price and we did that. By paying us on time you are returning that trust.

Responses for Business debt:

Because payment is expected on time we factor that into our pricing. Because of that our pricing saves you money and we feel it is only fair that we are paid on time.

I know you understand we need you to pay us so we can pay our bills. But we can't be your bank.

Debtor excuse: The check is in the mail

Consumer and business debt:

Great! When did you mail it? Where did you mail it, to what address, how much was it for? What is the check number?

If the date they give you was too long ago, ask for a new check now over the phone. Let them know that you will return the first check to them if it arrives at your office. This is also a good time to make sure the check is for the full amount due and not a partial payment. I say this based on my experience of learning that you must ask this question. When I first started out collecting I did not ask that question and more than once would receive a check as they had stated but it was for a much smaller amount than what was due. This becomes very frustrating, so be sure to ask the question and verify that the check amount is for the full balance due. If the check is NOT for the full balance due, now is the time for you to make specific arrangements for the repayment of the balance due. Then hang up and send the confirmation letter.

If someone gives you the objection that the product was not as promised or not what they had wanted or the wrong size or any type of problem with the service or merchandise some responses could be:

I wish you had notified us of this before the invoice became past due. Why haven't you contacted us about this?

What exactly is wrong with the service/product? Once they tell you the problem, let them know you will look into it right away and call them back. Go find out where the problem lies and get it resolved or come up with a resolution so you can call the customer back. If the claim is unjustified, some of the things you could say are:

I carefully reviewed your account and we show that you ordered product # and we shipped product # exactly as you had ordered it.

OR

I carefully reviewed your account and we show that product # are $3.00 each and with your discount, we charge you $2.48 each, which is also reflected on your PO#1234.

If you can provide me with something to show you did not order part#, which is on your PO#, and was shipped to you on bill #, we can investigate this further.

One of the most common excuses is to be told that someone never received the invoice or the bill in the mail. Some things you could reply with could be:

We mailed you an invoice inside the package that held your order; did you receive your order?

If they say they did not receive the order, ask them why they hadn't notified you, especially once they received your invoice for an order they did not receive. Tell them you will contact the shipper for a proof of delivery and call them back. You can also take this time to verify their shipping address.

We sent you an invoice and several statements, let me verify your mailing address and send you another right now.

I sent the invoice to your attention by certified mail and assumed you had received it by now, since you signed for it on DATE. Can you mail a check for the full amount today?

Find out if you can have the invoice delivered by messenger and ask them to have a check waiting for the messenger.

We mailed the invoice to – repeat their mailing address – which is the same address we have been mailing invoices to you for 5 years, has your address changed recently? (Insert how many years you have been using that address)

If it is a local customer, send someone or tell them you will be right over or stop by on your lunch break and pick it up. I have done this successfully and have found in most cases if they know when you are coming they will leave the check with the cashier or front office and be out to lunch or avoid seeing you. This still works and you get paid and it does cut down on problems with the customer in the future. It has been my experience that once you do this they really don't want you to do it again and so they avoid this situation by paying on time.

Working in business to business collections you know that a common excuse is that the purchase order and the invoice don't match up. If this happens to you ask them:

What exactly doesn't match?

If it is an error on your end, fix it and call them back to let them know it was a mistake and that you have corrected it. Send an invoice and give them short terms to pay it. Call them a few days after mailing the invoice just to make sure they received it, as a customer service call not a collection call.

If it is something that doesn't match that is minor and insignificant tell them you can send a corrected invoice but in the meantime can they process it for payment?

Another favourite excuse or stall tactic is I'm not sure, I will have to check my records and get back to you, or my husband has the check book and he isn't home. When this happens you don't want to hang up while they check – try to stay on the phone! If they put you off, call back in 30 minutes, and in another hour after that. If they don't respond by the next business day morning, call again and let them know you cannot wait any longer, they are not cooperating and you have to escalate the account. Let them know what action will be taken, for example, that could be reporting the debt to the credit bureau, revoking their credit limit, putting their other orders on hold etc.

If the debtor is someone you have done business with for years and have never been a problem before and they tell you this, give them the time to check their records but give them a specific date and time that you will call back for the update. If this is a customer or debtor that pays late often and you may have had to call before, make a specific date and time to call back and ask them if they will be there to take your call at that time on that date. This is very important, in my experience in doing this, many times someone will say they will be there at a specific time but then are not. Remember that each time a customer breaks a trust by not doing something they told you they would do to resolve the account, you need to escalate the account. Otherwise you will be calling this same account about this same balance for months. You want to move things along and get to the next account. Your job is to resolve the issue by either getting the bill paid or taking the steps needed when they don't pay and then moving on. Do not keep old past due balances on your books for years.

When asking them if they will be there and having them confirm, only to call and have them not be there, my next step or way to escalate the account was to make a personal visit if possible. If it was not possible for me to make a personal visit I could sometimes ask someone from a satellite office to visit a customer for me. If you have that capability, it works very well. You normally only have to do it once.

You can also ask what exactly they have to check in their records and let them know the invoice numbers, amounts due, total balance and ask what else they need. Offer to have someone stop by and pick up the check.

In a down economy more businesses have to make collection calls and more people have a harder time paying their bills. If a business account tells you they can't pay you because their customers aren't paying them, there are some things you can do. I have had this happen to me when I was making collection calls and it can be turned into a win-win situation for you and your customer by offering help to them in collecting their receivables.

If a customer tells you they can't pay you because their customers don't pay them, you could reply with:

Are your customers not paying you or just paying you slower?

Which customers, all of them, bigger customers?

What are you doing to collect from them?

Have you looked into a bank loan?

What exactly is the problem, maybe I can help.

At least some of your customers are still paying you, can you send me $100 today?

You are able to pay some of your bills, your phone is still connected, can you send me $100 today?

You can also offer suggestions to educational debt collection information you may have used and tell them it helped you. Let them know how you got out of the same situation. If they can relate to you in this way, you increase your chance of getting paid before someone who can't relate.

Sales and Credit departments seem to clash everywhere I have worked. The sales department wants to sell as much as they can but then the credit department is left trying to collect if they oversell and the customer can't pay. I have had customers tell me that their salesman told them not to worry about the past due balance when I called. If that happens to you, you could say:

Who is your sales representative?

When did he/she tell you this?

What exactly did they tell you?

You can also let them know that the salesman has no authority over changing their payment terms, explain to them that they signed a credit application or contract, they received the product or service and the invoice with the terms of sale clearly printed on them. Can I take your payment now over the phone?

If you get the response that the person you need to talk to is not in, you could say:

Could I speak to her supervisor/assistant/the owner of the company?

Who else can I speak to about this right now?

I left a message earlier and yesterday, I haven't had a call back and I can't keep extending the due date on this invoice. Can you please have her call me within the next hour or two because I have to discuss this with my supervisor later?

Another common response to your call is that the person who handles that is not in or they tell you the book keeper or accountant handles that. If you get this response ask for the name of the book keeper and their direct line or extension, ask if the book keeper is the one who issues the checks. Ask to be transferred but only after getting the name and direct number so that if you are disconnected you can call back.

If you call a customer and are told they are deceased offer your condolences and ask if you should call back in a few days or if they can talk now. You can wait until the next call or start with some questions during this call depending on how upset the person on the phone is.

Who should I speak to at this point? This could be an attorney, a family member or another person. When you do speak to whoever is handling the deceased estate you will want to make sure to have the full name and address of the estates administrator, the status of the estate, the names of anyone running a business if there was a business involved, details on any insurance policy.

If you call a customer and they can't help you because the computer is down ask them:

How long before it is back up?

When is the next check run scheduled? If they don't know or can't check ask them to write you a manual check.

What to avoid when making collection calls

Whenever you call any customer, no matter why you are calling, there are things you should never say. Always treat the customer how you would like to be treated if you were in the same situation. Your job is to get paid not alienate a customer who will then bad mouth your company all over town.

Making debt collection calls is a hard job; most people don't do it because it is their lifelong dream. If you are going to start calling people about debts as part of your job or as your primary job, you need to understand all aspects so that you can be effective without getting worn down. Making collection calls can be a thankless job and you need to have some protection. The most important thing to remember is that this is your job, you are doing a job, there is nothing personal going on, don't read into phone calls or get pulled into an emotionally charged conversation, let it go and move on to the next call.

Since this is a high stress job, you need to be able to relax, get up and walk around and stretch, and leave your job at the office. Clearing your head is crucial to being a good bill collector. We all see the news programs playing the recordings of a threatening message a bill collector is leaving for a debtor, but we never hear the threatening messages that debtors leave for bill collectors. I have been threatened many times on the phone and in person, I have had to have a police escort to my car after work at night due to threats. I have had to have irate customers removed from my office. Don't take threats lightly and take precautions for your physical safety as well as your mental sanity.

Making collection calls is emotionally draining. Mix it up with breaks, walks and doing something else for a little while if you have a particularly stressful call, then move on.

When you are making collection calls something else to avoid is having any questions about the collection laws where you are collecting. Have a copy of the laws on your desk and study them and know them inside and out. The best way to be effective when making collection calls is to know your stuff.

The top things to avoid when you are ready to make debt collection calls are important; knowing what they are so that you can avoid them will only make you a better collector. Always make sure you are calling at appropriate or allowed times, be conscious of the times zone where you are calling.

Avoid not being prepared, take a look at the customer's account before you call and make sure you understand the notes and know what is going on with the account so you can make a direct call for action. In my experience a call can be derailed when you are not prepared and the customer has a more current update on their account than you do and you end up having to hang up, look into it further and then get back to them.

Avoid being too easy, that is avoid letting the debtor talk you into allowing them to pay a minimal amount with no firm schedule of payment for the entire past due amount. For example, a debtor may tell you what financial problems they have run into which has caused them to become past due with you. Then they may tell you that all they can do is send you $20 now and they don't know when they can pay more. Some collectors just say OK at this point and hang up. This is behaviour to avoid, keep talking to the customer to find out more about their finances, when they get paid, and ask for more than what they offer and set up firm payments for the balance. For example, they will send you $50 today, then $50 every Friday for 1 month at which time you will call them to re-evaluate their financial situation and hopefully raise the payment. I have done this many times with success. The first call when you set up the payments, usually goes pretty well and the customer agrees to everything. When I would hang up with them, I would send them a letter outlining each payment and when it was due, I was very specific including the dates and new balance. Getting the second payment isn't always as easy, and you may get each one but with a little work and follow up, when you try to re-negotiate the amount of the payment after that one month period, that is when I would run into resistance. Another thing that worked for me in this situation was to come back after the second payment or when I was calling about the second payment and offer to lower the payment by $10. Many times that is all it took for the customer to start making the payment regularly without me having to call and spend time and money trying to get them to pay. Sometimes people have a hard time coming up with a certain amount but if you just lower it a little it can be more realistic for them and help you both out.

Avoid missing a payment over the phone opportunity. Getting paid over the phone right away is always better than waiting for a check. I have seen collectors avoid even mentioning accepting a payment over the phone or online and when I have asked them about it, they wave their hand and say, "Oh that's ok; they are just sending a check". No, that is not ok, if you can get payment over the phone and resolve that account right now, you need to do that. To do this make sure you are aware of the many different payment options your business offers. You can accept credit or debit card payments, checks over the phone, maybe a way to pay online using a credit or debit card or PayPal type services. Many customers prefer to pay online so make sure this option is available to them and is easy for them to use. You will thank yourself.

The biggest thing to avoid when making collection calls is losing your emotional side during the call. Making collection calls can be emotionally draining, some of the emotions you will feel when making collection calls include boredom, when someone is going on and on about their life, their finances and why they can't pay you. Annoyance and Frustration with follow up calls to customers who don't seem to be taking this situation seriously. Sadness when you talk to a customer who is in a particularly sensitive situation from death, divorce, loss of home, job or income. Anger when a customer flat out lies to you, again. Extreme anger when a customer acts like a jerk, is demeaning, yells at you or swears at you and calls you names. Exasperation when you take a payment over the phone only to hang up and find the check won't clear, or is a closed account or the credit card is denied. As the collector it is up to you to have compassion and understanding but to remember the goal of your call and stay focused. You can be sorry for someone's situation and offer help but ultimately you are calling to help them find a way to pay you.

As you talk on the phone avoid mumbling and avoid not smiling, a smile can be heard in your voice. This is a small easy thing that you can do that will help you be a better collector. Avoid slumping over your computer looking at customer accounts, and mumbling into your phone. Speak up, you don't want to make this call, the person on the other end doesn't want to talk about this, be clear so you can get through the call and move on. Don't be so unclear or talk too softly so that you have to repeat yourself.

When someone is telling you their story and maybe going on a bit, don't get distracted and stop paying attention or check your email or do anything else. When I was in that situation I would start trying to think of things to say to get back to setting up payments, talking about something they said about a job or borrowing money. Many times a debtor will cry and vent and still be nice on the phone and promise a payment that never comes.

When to set up payment arrangements

Print out a current accounts receivable listing and look at your customers' accounts, what they owe, how much they owe, how old it is, their payment history and when was the last time their credit limit was reviewed? Once you see this information, you will notice which customers might need to set up a payment arrangement. Some things to look for are larger balances due than in the past, they are taking longer to pay now than they have been in the past, they have stopped ordering from you and paying you. If you notice any of these things, now is the time to set up payment arrangements with those customers and customers who might be past due in general or are due now but you haven't received a check.

You should think about setting up payment arrangements when you find yourself unable to pay your own bills on time, or you find your daily deposits are much smaller than they have been or when you find that your customers are not paying like they have in the past. It is important to stay on top of these things and start offering payment plans before any of these things becomes a bigger problem. Nipping cash flow issues in the bud is a very important part of payment plans.
How to set up payment arrangements

You only need to set up payment arrangements if a customer cannot make payment in full. You must always make the arrangement by talking with the customer, and then you MUST follow up by sending a written notice or letter reiterating what that arrangement is. The only way to make this work is to be very specific. The first line of your letter should say something like, "As per our conversation today and put the date of the call" then go on to state the terms you agreed to, the total due, the number of payments, the due date of each payment and the amount of each payment, I cannot stress enough that you need to be very specific. Also, include a payment envelope if you can, because the easier you make it for the customer to pay, the better your chances are of getting paid.

Never start a call with a customer by asking them how much they can pay; this is just setting you up for failure. To be in control of the call you must let the customer know how much you can accept not the other way around. Once you ask the debtor how much they can pay, you lose all negotiations and you lose control of the call and the situation.

Some of you are new to setting up payment arrangements or might even be new to calling the customers. It is essential to communicate confidence when you are speaking to past due customers. You must be relaxed, confident, and prepared. Remember, everything you do represents your company: How you speak, how you collect money, send out invoices, and handle tough situations. Some things to consider when speaking to customers and making payments arrangements:

First impressions – When your customer realizes you are calling about a past due invoice, they will not be happy. You must portray confidence, smile when you speak into the phone, it will be noticeable in your voice.

Your voice should be loud enough to be heard and sound confident, not to loud but not too soft. You want your customer to hear you and understand everything you are saying. Sit up straight in your chair and imagine this person is sitting across from you.

Maintain "eye contact" by staying focused on the call. Don't check your email or watch the other people in your office. Stay focused.

Relax! Sit up straight in your chair; don't play with paperclips or pens on your desk. Use your face, voice, and posture to send your confidence over the phone and in person.

If you put these techniques into effect, you will collect more money and have better results from the calls you make. Take steps to ensure you make your calls in the most effective way the first time, so you don't have to continue to make calls to people that you let have control of the situation.

When deciding how to set up each customer on their specific payment plan, decide how many monthly payments you can extend to the customer, divide the total amount due by the number of months you want the balance to be paid in. This will be the monthly payment.

Make sure when you set up a payment arrangement with any customer that you PUT IT IN WRITING. This is very important. Let the customer know that if they cannot make a payment, to call you and let you know, don't just skip the payment because this could void the payment agreement. This way you will keep the lines of communication open with your customer, while helping them to stay on track and keeping some cash flow through your business.

Steps for successful payment arrangements

1. Ask for payment in full.
2. If the customer cannot pay in full, offer to split the balance due into two payments.
3. If that is not possible, it is time to negotiate by gathering more information on the customers' financial status.
4. Ask open ended questions so you can evaluate the situation.
5. Suggest weekly or bi-monthly payments, as opposed to the common monthly payments.
6. Come to an agreement that is beneficial to you and the customer.
7. Get a commitment and document it.
8. Send the customer a letter reiterating your understanding of the agreement.
9. Ask for a signature on the agreement.

Always start off asking for the payment in full, then go down from there. Always aim high, such as first asking for 100% then 80% then 75% etc. If you leave it up to the customer they will offer the lowest possible amount and that may not help you in your situation at all and certainly won't help them. Based on the economy and how it stands now, you may have to get some pretty small payments but try to get as much as you can as frequently as you can.

- Send a confirmation letter the day you make the payment arrangement with the customer.
- Send a payment reminder 10 days before the payment is due.
- On the due date if you do not have payment, send a letter giving them 5 days to pay before the arrangement is revoked and they go back to full collections on the full amount.

Another example might be that once you have the owner of the business or the debtor on the phone, identify yourself and your company and state the purpose of your call. If the person tells you they cannot pay

anything, listen to them and ask specific questions to help you offer a solution to the debtor.
You might ask things such as:

- Do you have a job?
- Does your spouse have a job?
- Are you collecting unemployment?
- When do you get paid?

Learn as much as you can about their financial situation and their other bills so you can help to offer a realistic payment plan. If your payment plan is not realistic, it will not happen.

Send a confirmation letter that day, confirming your conversation and the date as well as all payment details. Include how much will be paid on which date and in how many payments, you might want to include what will happen if the arrangements are not met. Offer to re-evaluate their payment arrangement if their financial situation changes.

To learn more about successful payment plans read "Using Payment Plans to Get Paid". http://www.amazon.com/Using-Payment-Plans-Collecting-Money-ebook/dp/B006ABH1B4/

Skills & resources needed for setting up payment plans

Anyone who is trying to collect money, even if the amount was agreed upon at the time of the sale, needs to know how to negotiate. Some skills needed to be a good negotiator:

Understanding the negotiation process – highly effective collectors recognize that negotiations are a process. It requires an understanding of the billing, credit approval and payment processes.

Focusing on a Win-Win situation – Win-win means that both parties feel like they have "won" during the collection process. Great bill collectors' help their customers try to solve problems and look for opportunities to make that possible. They also know when to be firm and limit what they do in order to reach an agreement that is acceptable for both parties.

Patience – Too many collectors try to go for the "quick fix" so they can get paid and move on to the next account. Good bill collectors know that patience is a virtue and that rushing the collection process only leads to not getting paid. Gather information BEFORE contacting your customer, then think carefully about possible solutions and this is really critical because major mistakes can be made when you rush.

Confidence – Good collectors are confident when making a call or writing a letter. They aren't arrogant, rude or cocky, they are confident and helpful. You must believe in your ability to reach a win-win agreement with the customer, this is obtained through experience.

Listening skills – People will tell you just about everything you need to know if you ask the right questions or keep quiet long enough for them to continue speaking. The biggest mistake a bill collector can make is not listening or bigger yet, interrupting a customer when that might mean if they had just listened longer, they may have received key information that would assist them in their collection effort. When you call a customer and you state the reason for your call or ask a question, wait for the answer. No matter how long the pause may be, let the customer break that silence with an answer.

Some other skills needed to be able to work with your customers to get paid, or set up payment arrangements are:

Managing the emotional side – customers will get upset that you are calling them. They have bigger and better things to think about other than your bill, they will cry, yell at you, hang up on you and swear at you. When a customer starts to tell you their life history and how this affects how they pay you, you need to be able to have some compassion but offer a solution to get the bill paid. This is when you would offer a payment plan or different payment options.

Prepare a pre-call plan: before you ever call a customer about their balance, you need to research their account. Before you dial, make sure you know the invoice number, date, amount that is past due, how past due it is, the payment history, details of the order and if there were any disputed items. When the customer asks you any question, you need to answer immediately whenever possible, otherwise you lose time and time is money.

Having an opening statement ready – your opening statement should be very brief and to the point. You need to identify yourself and your company, state why you are calling and what you want.

For example:

"Hi, this is Michelle from KTM Auto calling about your past due balance of $500.00 on invoice #1234 dated 4/1/08. I am calling today to take your payment over the phone to clear this balance from your account. Would you like to pay with a credit or debit card or check by phone?"

STOP

WAIT for an answer and always assume the debtor will pay. This is the point where they may tell you they can't pay in full and you would proceed to start setting up a payment plan.

Ask questions – asking questions with precision and making the transition to the payment arrangement – all your questions should be clear and to the point with silence after each question, so the customer can answer.

Make sure you LISTEN.

For example:

Customer: I can't pay, I don't have any money.

You: Are you working?
Customer: Yes, but I just started a job and don't get paid for 2 weeks.

You: What day will you get paid?

Customer: Friday

You: Okay, we can accept a payment of half the balance on Saturday.

This can go on and on, the customer might then tell you they can't pay half, you work down from there until you reach a realistic agreement. Then send out a confirmation letter with all the details of the agreement. Then you call on Friday to remind them about making that payment.

For example:

"Hi this is Michelle from KTM Auto calling to confirm you will be mailing your check for $50 tomorrow, Saturday as we agreed."

Anyone working with your customers to set up payment arrangements needs to:

- Be interest in people, and be a good communicator both verbally and in writing.
- Be persuasive and persistent, with the sensitivity to deal fairly with people in often difficult situations.
- Be able to stay calm under pressure, and be adaptable in sometimes tricky situations.
- Have strong negotiation skills and the ability to explain financial matters firmly and clearly.
- Have mathematical ability to explain payments, financial terms and credit services and policies.
- Be able to understand relevant legislation concerning data protection and harassment.
- Have office administration and computer skills.

Elements of a payment plan

1. Contact is made with the customer.
2. You ask for payment in full, the customer lets you know that is not possible and asks for a payment plan.
3. You ask the debtor basic questions regarding their finances
   a. Are you working?
   b. Is your spouse/significant other/roommate working?
   c. When do you get paid?
   d. What other debts do you have to pay? (Credit cards, car payments, day care etc.)
   e. Are you receiving unemployment?
   f. How are you paying your bills now?
   g. What is your profession or what do you do?
   h. How much do you make an hour or week?
4. Ask questions that will help you to determine the approximate disposable income of the customer.
5. Depending on the amount of income the customer has and the amount owed, make a realistic estimate on what you would like to ask for in terms of monthly, weekly, bi-weekly etc, payments.
6. Offer more than one option to the customer so they have a part in the decision and are more likely to make those payments.

In conclusion I would like to remind you that so many business owners and third party debt collection agencies, do not take all of these steps or even some of these steps. I have shared with you actual and specific steps I have taken in my years of doing collection work, which have worked well for me. I have found that when making collection calls and dealing with excuses, you must be firm, tread lightly, have compassion and treat the account carefully. Treat the account (not the customer) like a child who needs your guidance and help to get this paid. This has worked very well for me and I have successfully collected more money than other collectors based on following these steps. I hope what I have shared with you in this book can help you collect more money and was helpful to you.

What is the FDCPA?

The Fair Debt Collection Practices Act is in place to eliminate debt collection abuse and to help debt collectors have guidelines to follow while protecting consumers as well as creditors.

The FDCPA puts restrictions on different debt collection practices that are done by a third party or collection agency. As of this writing debt collectors are allowed to contact a debtor in person, by mail, by telephone, by telegram and by fax.

Not many people use telegrams anymore but we do use technology and none of this is listed there since the FDCPA has not been updated as of the time of this writing.

Third party collectors are restricted from contacting debtors at inconvenient times or places. Third party collectors are prohibited from contacting debtors at their place of employment if the agency is aware that the debtor's employer disapproves of this action. Third party collectors are prohibited from certain harassing or abusive practices.

The **Fair Debt Collection Practices Act (FDCPA)** is a United States statute added in 1978 as part of the Consumer Credit Protection Act. Its purposes are to eliminate abusive practices in the collection of consumer debts, to promote fair debt collection and to provide consumers with an avenue for disputing and obtaining validation of debt information in order to ensure the information's accuracy. The Act creates guidelines under which debt collectors may conduct business, defines rights of consumers involved with debt collectors, and prescribes penalties and remedies for violations of the Act. It is sometimes used in conjunction with the Fair Credit Reporting Act.

A debt under the FDCPA is an obligation to pay money for things which are used for personal, family or household use. A debt does not have to be a judgment in order to be a debt.

It is important to note that no agency has the authority to issue regulations under the FDCPA until the passage of the Dodd-Frank Act vested that authority in the CFPB, Director Rich Cordray has issued a statement illustrating the CFPB's intent to modernize the application of the statute through the CFPB's planned regulations because the "existing measures that were written before the Internet, social media, and before many other new technologies."

The CFPB is a federal regulator, and as they continue their rulemaking, they take industry silence as assent. Consumers are speaking out, complaining and making their voice heard, as part of the debt collection industry, if we want these rules to be fair we must also make our voices heard. This includes debt buyers, collection attorneys and using newer technologies to communicate and social media.

To learn more check out the FDCPA text online at www.ftc.gov and read "Understanding and Following the FDCPA" http://www.amazon.com/Understanding-Collection-Practices-Collecting-Series-ebook/dp/B006UGYRBQ/

Resources

Free credit applications http://www.michelledunn.com/free.html

A Free Collection Guide e-book http://michelledunn.com/free-from-michelle

Books, Special Reports and more at http://www.MichelleDunn.com and "Tipping the Scales" e-book by Tim Paulsen http://www.trpaulsen.com/tippingthescales.html

More books by Michelle to help you collect more money: http://www.amazon.com/s/ref=ntt_athr_dp_sr_1?_encoding=UTF8&search-alias=digital-text&field-author=Michelle%20Dunn

Effective collections tutorials: http://www.youtube.com/user/MichelleDunn1?feature=mhee

My Credit and collections blog: http://www.Credit-and-Collections.com

Fair Debt Collection Practices Act: http://www.ftc.gov

Networking groups:

The Guide to Getting Paid group: http://www.linkedin.com/groups/Guide-Getting-Paid-2652085?trk=myg_ugrp_ovr

Starting a Collection Agency group: http://www.linkedin.com/groups/Starting-Collection-Agency-2320092?gid=2320092&trk=hb_side_g

Credit & Collections email discussion group: http://finance.groups.yahoo.com/group/creditandcollections/

Visit my Facebook page often for announcements of FREE offers on all of my Kindle titles and articles and tips to help you collect more money and prevent bad debt: http://www.facebook.com/pages/The-Guide-to-Getting-Paid/175893280661

Collection Letter Secrets to Getting Paid - http://sbinformation.about.com/od/bizlettersamples/a/debtcollection.htm

10 Free Sample Business Collection Letters – (7th item down) http://sbinformation.about.com/od/bizlettersamples/Business_Letter_Samples_Business_Letter_Writing.htm

Listing of Excuses and actual conversations in great detail can be found in the The Ultimate Credit & Collections Handbook, in chapter 14 pages 116-119. http://www.amazon.com/Ultimate-Credit-Collections-Handbook-Michelle/dp/1599180251/sr=1-2/qid=1172066411/ref=sr_1_2/102-2301573-3180946?ie=UTF8&s=books

About the author

A 27 year debt collection industry veteran, entrepreneur, award winning author, self-syndicated columnist, one of the Top 5 Women in Collections and one of the Top 50 most influential collection professionals in her industry, Michelle Dunn is the author of many books. Learn more at www.Credit-and-Collections.com & www.MichelleDunn.com

Books that can help you collect more money

Please connect with me on LinkedIn and follow me on Twitter

 www.LinkedIn.com/in/creditmd

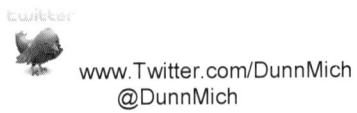 www.Twitter.com/DunnMich
@DunnMich

www.Credit-and-Collections.com

www.MichelleDunn.com

Thank you for buying my book! If you felt it was helpful to you, it would be helpful to me if you would leave me a review on Amazon.com.

Thank you! – *Michelle Dunn*

23973375R00033

Printed in Great Britain
by Amazon